# Pricing for Profit

Steven M. Bragg

**AccountingTools®**

ISBN 978-1-64221-272-3

# Table of Contents

**Chapter 1 - Pricing for Profit** ...........................................................1

*Introduction* ...........................................................................*1*

*Senior Management Support* ..........................................................*1*

*The Impact of a Price Increase* ......................................................*1*

    Breakeven Volume for a Price Increase .........................................2

*The Optimum Price Point* ..............................................................*3*

*The Low-Price Mindset* .................................................................*4*

*The Concept of the Committed Buyer* ...............................................*5*

*The Value Premium* ......................................................................*6*

    Market Segmentation to Enhance the Value Premium .......................7

    The Value Pricing Approach .....................................................8

    The Dissipation of Value Over Time.............................................9

    Value Pricing Sales Techniques .................................................9

*Transactional Pricing Adjustments* ................................................*10*

    Charge for Free Services .......................................................11

*Price Increase Experimentation* ....................................................*12*

*Eliminate Unprofitable Customers* .................................................*12*

*Product Line Pricing* ..................................................................*16*

*The Use of Bundling* ...................................................................*16*

*Offer Options* ..........................................................................*18*

*Discount Avoidance* ....................................................................*19*

*Loss Leader Adjustments* .............................................................*20*

*Monitor Market Capacity* .............................................................*21*

*Other Factors Impacting Your Prices* ..............................................*21*

*Install Proper Price Administration* ...............................................*22*

*How to Reduce Prices* .................................................................*23*

*The Frequency of Pricing Discussions* .............................................*23*

*Summary*.................................................................................*24*

**Chapter 2 - Constraint-Based Pricing** ...........................................**25**

*Introduction*............................................................................*25*

*Pricing Strategies*......................................................................*25*

    Cost-Based Pricing Strategies .................................................25

    Value Pricing Strategies .........................................................26

Teaser Pricing Strategies ...............................................................26

Strategic Pricing ...........................................................................26

*Constraint Analysis Financial Terminology*.................................27

*Constraint Analysis from a Financial Perspective* ......................27

*The Constraint Analysis Model* ...................................................28

*The Decision to Sell at a Lower Price* .........................................31

*Price Modeling* .............................................................................32

*Pricing for a Lengthy Setup Time* ...............................................32

*The Decision to Enter into a Long-Term Contract*.......................32

*Pricing When There is no Constraint Impact* ..............................33

*Dealing with a Market Constraint*...............................................34

*Objections to Constraint-Based Pricing*......................................36

*Summary*.......................................................................................37

**Chapter 3 - Target Costing**.............................................................**38**

*Introduction* ..................................................................................38

*The Basic Steps of Target Costing*...............................................38

*Value Engineering Considerations*..............................................40

*The Cost Reduction Program* ......................................................41

*The Milestone Review Process* .....................................................41

*Problems with Target Costing*......................................................42

*The Members of a Design Team* ...................................................43

*The Role of the Accountant in Target Costing*.............................44

*Data Sources for Target Costing*..................................................45

*The Product Life Cycle and Target Costing* ................................46

*Summary*.......................................................................................46

**Glossary**...........................................................................................**48**

**Index** ................................................................................................**49**

# About the Author

**Steven Bragg, CPA,** has been the chief financial officer or controller of four companies, as well as a consulting manager at Ernst & Young. He received a master's degree in finance from Bentley College, an MBA from Babson College, and a Bachelor's degree in Economics from the University of Maine. He has been a two-time president of the Colorado Mountain Club, and is an avid alpine skier, mountain biker, and certified master diver. Mr. Bragg resides in Centennial, Colorado. He has written more than 300 books and courses, including *New Controller Guidebook*, *GAAP Guidebook*, and *Payroll Management*. He has also written *The Auditors* science fiction trilogy.

Steven maintains the accountingtools.com web site, which contains continuing professional education courses, the Accounting Best Practices podcast, and thousands of articles on accounting subjects.

---

### Buy Additional AccountingTools Courses

AccountingTools offers more than 1,500 hours of CPE courses, with concentrations in accounting, auditing, finance, taxation, and ethics. Related courses that you might like include:

- CFO Guidebook
- Effective Sales Forecasting
- Effective Sales Management
- Revenue Management

Go to accountingtools.com/cpe to view these additional courses.

AccountingTools®

---

# Chapter 1
# Pricing for Profit

## Introduction

Many business owners feel that they are trapped by prevailing market prices, and cannot price their goods and services any higher. This is not always the case. In this book, we discuss the mindset that leads people to feel boxed in by the current market price, and what tools are available for understanding the true value of what they are selling – as well as the real prices that can be charged. This can result in a significant profit boost, without having to increase your unit volume at all. In later chapters, we will address other ways to price for profit, with a particular emphasis on constraint-based pricing.

## Senior Management Support

The concepts that we will address in this book must be supported by the senior management team. The reason is that some departments tend to work against pricing increases, resulting in an ongoing profit deterioration. For example, the marketing department may want to pursue a lowest-price strategy in order to increase market share, while individual salespeople are willing to cut pricing deals with their customers in order to secure sales. Even the accounting department can interfere with pricing by offering customers early payment discounts that can significantly reduce profit levels. Consequently, the senior management team must impose ongoing pressure on the entire organization to ensure that prices are set at levels that optimize profits.

> **Tip:** Have someone specifically in charge of pricing. Otherwise, pricing initiatives tend to get lost in the scrum of daily management activities. Pricing should be this person's central task, so there is no excuse for inattention to pricing optimization. Also, the person put in charge of pricing should be sufficiently senior to carry real weight within the organization, so that department heads understand that senior management is serious about maintaining robust pricing.

A key responsibility for the senior management team is absolving the sales staff from blame if a price increase causes some customers to take their business elsewhere. Otherwise, salespeople will be taking the blame for lost revenues that were triggered by the pricing demands of the management team.

## The Impact of a Price Increase

You can generate a remarkable profit boost from even a small bump in prices. This is because there are no incremental costs associated with a price increase, other than a credit card fee (if customers are paying in this manner) and the income tax on any resulting profit increase. The following exhibit reveals the profit amounts that could be generated from a 1% price increase for businesses of different sizes. While the benefit is modest for a smaller business, it can be remarkable for a larger one.

**Profits Resulting from a 1% Price Increase**

| Current Revenue Level | $1 Million | $5 Million | $25 Million |
|---|---|---|---|
| 1% revenue increase | $10,000 | $50,000 | $250,000 |
| Credit card fee @ 3.5% | -350 | -1,750 | -8,750 |
| Taxable margin | 9,650 | 48,250 | 241,250 |
| Income tax @ 21%* | -2,027 | -10,133 | -50,663 |
| Net profit increase | $7,623 | $38,117 | $190,587 |
| Percent return | 76% | 76% | 76% |

\* Federal tax rate. No state income tax is included, since some states do not impose one.

As the exhibit reveals, it is quite reasonable to expect a 76% percent return on any price increase. Given the potential profit impact of even a slight increase in price, doesn't it make sense to explore how this might be achieved?

**Breakeven Volume for a Price Increase**

While the preceding discussion of profits resulting from a price increase looks tempting, you also need to consider the potential loss of profits if customers leave as a result of a price increase. There is a formula for this, which focuses on determining the breakeven sales volume at which you will continue to generate your existing profit. The formula is:

Breakeven sales volume = (Percent change in price) ÷ (Percent variable margin + Percent change in price)

For example, if you are considering a 5% price increase on a 35% variable-margin product, the breakeven sales volume will be:

Breakeven sales volume = (-5%) ÷ (35% variable margin + 5% change in price)

Breakeven sales volume = 12.5%

In short, if you raise prices by 5% at the indicated variable margin level, then you can afford to lose up to 12.5% of your sales volume before your profitability begins to decline. If the sales volume decline is less than 12.5%, then your profits will increase.

This calculation brings up the issue of how pricing adjustments would impact a very high-margin business (such as software products), or a very low-margin business (such as commodity products). Let's start with a high-margin business that generates 70% margins. A 5% change in prices results in the following calculation:

Breakeven sales volume = (-5%) ÷ (70% variable margin + 5% change in price)

Breakeven sales volume = 6.7%

Then let's use the same 5% price increase for a business that only generates a 5% margin. The calculation is:

Breakeven sales volume = (-5%) ÷ (5% variable margin + 5% change in price)

Breakeven sales volume = 50%

In short, a high-margin business needs to be very careful about raising its prices further, because it is already generating such a large return on each dollar of sales generated; if it loses even a few customers, this can have a notable negative effect on its profits. Conversely, a low-margin business is well-advised to experiment with price increases, since doing so can massively increase its bottom line – even at the cost of quite a few lost customers.

> **Tip:** If you operate a high-margin business where there is a significant downside risk to boosting prices and losing customers, consider imposing very small, incremental price increases over time. This allows you to edge up towards the maximum price that customers will tolerate, and quite possibly without any of them noticing the change.

## The Optimum Price Point

Is there such a thing as an optimum price point, where you can generate the maximum amount of profit? Economics professors would lead you to believe that this is the case, and can easily produce a chart that shows such a "sweet spot." In reality, this is a shifting target that is impacted by many factors, including the following:

- *Changes in the mix of competitors and their offerings*. For example, new entrants from super-low-cost Chinese firms may shift price points down so far that no amount of branding will offset this advantage.
- *Changes in customer tastes*. For example, the purveyors of branded jeans know that fickle customers may stop buying their wares entirely, as soon as a new style is introduced by someone else.
- *Changes in technology*. For example, the desirability of cars has shifted, depending on whether they have any number of whizzy new technological features built into them.

- *Changes in the products offered in adjacent markets.* For example, the market for flashlights was destroyed when cell phones were introduced that had built-in LED lights.
- *Changes in the income levels of customers.* For example, the market for luxury goods is negatively impacted whenever the stock market declines, because its richest customers now find themselves with a lower net worth.

In short, finding the optimum price point is extremely difficult, and once reached, it may only last for a short period of time, after which it shifts.

## The Low-Price Mindset

Many business owners feel that they cannot price their products higher than the prevailing market rate, especially when they are competing against big, well-known brands. Their logic appears to be that branded products have a higher-quality image, so the only option left is to set prices lower. This logic skips one notable piece of analysis, which is what expenditure would be required to lift the value of an organization's brand to the point where an offsetting increase in prices could be justified? In many cases, this expenditure is relatively small. Examples of reasonably-priced brand upgrades are as follows:

- Re-jigger the product packaging to give the impression of a higher-quality product
- Advertise where committed customers are most likely to see it
- Pay social media influencers to mention your products
- Sponsor events that your most committed customers attend
- Post favorable product reviews and testimonials
- Issue occasional press releases about your products
- Issue an email newsletter to long-term customers
- Commission a new tagline that highlights the best features of the product
- Over time, redesign your products so that they have a common look and feel

In short, there are numerous ways to improve your branding without spending an inordinate amount of money. By making the right investments in the right branding activities, you can convey a value level to customers that will justify a higher price.

In addition, you can make several operational improvements that will improve your brand. Here are several examples:

- Increase the speed and/or convenience of order placements
- Increase the percentage of complete orders shipped within one day of order placement
- Invest in more product development
- Increase your product quality in areas where customers have complained in the past

Of the preceding operational improvements, pay particular attention to product development. If you can create a truly unique product, you may be able to charge far more for it to early adopters, who are typically willing to pay much more than price-sensitive consumers. Of course, this premium will only last until all early adopters have purchased the product, at which point you will need to lower the price to attract all other buyers.

> **Tip:** If you feel that a price discount is absolutely required to get new customers to sample your product, then make quite clear that the discount is only good for a short period of time. This keeps customers from expecting you to offer low pricing all the time. This is an especially good approach for a new company that has to offer a good deal to gain customers.

Business owners may also feel that customers value a low price more than anything else, because that is always their key negotiating point; they are always badgering the firm about whether it can sell at a lower price. Consider why this is the case; if you have done a poor job of branding, then customers do not know how your services differ from those of your competitors, and so will concentrate on the only thing left – which is the price. If you do a proper job of branding, then customers will understand your value proposition, and will place less emphasis on obtaining a reduced price.

> **Tip:** If your customers are solely interested in obtaining the lowest price, then they likely have no loyalty to you at all. If someone else offers them a better deal, then they will take their business elsewhere. Are these the customers you want? It would be better not to cater to this group, and instead pursue customers who value good service and a higher-quality product. If this initially results in 100% customer turnover, then so be it – the new group of customers will be much more loyal that the departing ones.

## The Concept of the Committed Buyer

A committed buyer is someone willing to pay a premium – however small – over the market price for a good or service. For example, some BMW drivers are willing to pay a substantial premium to own one of these cars – as is the case for afficionados who dote on their Porsches and Bentleys. While these examples might indicate that only wealthy individuals are committed enough to pay a premium, this is not always the case. For example, a low-income person might be such a committed camper that he will spend an inordinate amount for ultra-light camping gear, while a low-income bicyclist might skimp elsewhere in order to afford a carbon fiber racing bike. Or, there is the buyer of fashion-label clothes, who might forgo purchasing a $15 tee shirt in favor of one with a famous brand label on it that is functionally the same, but which costs ten times more.

Committed buyers tend to concentrate their biggest purchases in highly targeted areas, where they care a great deal about what they are purchasing. In all other areas, they will likely do whatever it takes to pay no more than the market price, and may even go to some lengths to purchase at below-market rates. The three areas in which committed buyers tend to focus their attention are as follows:

- *On products that save them time.* Tends to be people who schedule every moment of their days, and who deeply value efficiency. For example, software that reduces the administrative time of salespeople would be greeted with cries of joy.
- *On products that have innovative features.* Tends to be people who are always experimenting with the latest models of their favorite toys (such as computers, televisions, or cars). This group can be subdivided into early adopters who are willing to pay a premium for the latest features, mainstream buyers, and laggards who only buy new product features after they have long since been adopted by others.
- *On products that will enhance their image.* Tends to be people who value their status with others, and who have a high regard for product quality.

For example, if you are selling a product to a potential customer who values efficiency more than anything else, then don't try to sell him a high-status item – this is a mismatch. Instead, your ideal committed customer is someone who has a high regard for the specific type of value that you are offering. This customer will be most willing to pay your stated price. If the customer's interests tend to focus on other areas, then you will have to offer a discount in order to secure the deal – resulting in a lower profit than might otherwise have been the case with the ideal committed customer.

> **Tip:** Create marketing messages that are most likely to attract those customers who are interested in your value proposition. Thus, if you are setting high price points and offering an extremely high-quality product, then only produce ads that focus on quality. Otherwise, you will attract customers who are not sufficiently committed to pay your elevated prices.

## The Value Premium

Pricing for profit involves setting price points that represent a reasonable premium over competing commodity-level offerings, but which are not so high that committed customers no longer see the value in your products. To ensure that customers *do* see this value, consider preparing marketing materials that communicate the value proposition provided by your products. These materials can be highly quantitative, specifying the savings that can be expected from using your product. In some cases, it may make sense to adopt value pricing for individual customers, if you can provide unique solutions for them that will generate a sufficiently robust return.

**EXAMPLE**

Unique Corporation has released a new electric car that includes solar cells on its roof. These cells reduce the average amount of time that the car must be plugged in by about 30 minutes per day in order to obtain a 100% battery recharge. The value created by this innovation is a reduction in the cost of the electricity that is no longer needed to charge the battery, which the company calculates to be $2 per day, or $730 per year. The company's pricing manager decides to increase the price of the car by $2,000 because of this feature, on the grounds that customers will be paid back after three years of daily use, after which the solar cells will generate a significant cost reduction for them.

A year later, the cost of electricity in the company's target market declines to the point where the electricity savings for customers declines to $1 per day. In order to continue providing a reasonable value premium to its customers, the pricing manager reduces the cost of the car by $1,000.

As indicated by the preceding example, you need to continually monitor the market price of alternative commodity products in order to set reasonable value premiums that make sense for customers. Otherwise, the value premium may eventually become untenable. This requires continual communication with the sales staff to understand the feedback they are receiving from customers about your product's value.

**Market Segmentation to Enhance the Value Premium**

A product feature may be considered quite valuable within one segment of a market, and minimally valuable in another segment. If you can recognize these features and the segments within which they are valuable, then it makes sense to market the product differently in each segment, and with a higher price point where the feature is valued more. This concept can be exploited heavily, as long as you can keep identifying additional market segments.

**EXAMPLE**

Granular Corporation manufactures a chemical that is primarily used as a paint thinner. As such, it is a commodity product, and can only be sold at a price of $10/gallon. However, a salesperson learns from a customer that it can also dissolve ice, and is being used on people's walkways and driveways in the winter. Granular accordingly repackages the chemical for this use, and raises the price to $20/gallon. The underlying product is exactly the same, but the targeted market segment is completely different, and has a much higher regard for the product.

## The Value Pricing Approach

Determining value pricing might initially appear to be quite difficult, since it requires a deep knowledge of the circumstances of each customer to which you intend to offer it. This is a multi-step process, but can be quite worthwhile if the result is a major profit boost. Here are the essential steps in the process:

1. Identify the next best alternative product for your customer that is being offered by a competitor. This represents the next lowest price that the customer will compare to your product.
2. Itemize every advantage that your product gives the customer over and above the competing offering. This might include such items as better quality, better service, more robust field service, or specific features.
3. Itemize every disadvantage that your product has relative to the competition, and only from the customer's perspective.
4. Quantify these advantages and disadvantages. This can be quite difficult for some features that are more qualitative (such as a better-looking product). The intent is to establish the incremental value of your product from the perspective of the customer over what is being offered by the competition.
5. Add these quantified advantages to the price being offered by the competition, and reduce the outcome by the quantified disadvantages of your product. The difference between your quantified outcome and the competitor's price is the value gap of your product to that customer.
6. Set a price for that customer that lies somewhere within the value gap, so that you are sharing some of the value with the customer. You have to give the customer some of this value gap, or else it will have no reason to buy your product.

This analysis may have to be conducted with individual customers, though this is only cost-effective if you can earn a sufficient premium to make it worth your administrative effort. More commonly, you would conduct it for a customer segment, where every customer in the segment faces roughly the same value proposition.

The preceding analysis is really tailored to either a specific customer or market segment. Consequently, when your salespeople are selling to a new customer, it is critical to assign it to the correct market segment. Otherwise, you may end up pricing your product incorrectly, based on a misperception about what the customer considers to be important.

---

**Tip:** It can be quite difficult to establish exactly what advantages your product has in the eyes of your customers, so it may be necessary to interview a number of them to gather this information. They may not be willing to talk, since they may suspect that the outcome will be an increase in the prices you charge, so be prepared to offer them a discount for a period of time in exchange for this information.

---

A value pricing analysis will need to be conducted on an ongoing basis, because two factors will change over time: the expectations of your customers regarding the value of your products, and the features of the competing product. The latter issue is likely to be more urgent, since it is quite possible that competitors will be continually trying to close the value gap.

> **Tip:** A value pricing analysis is most worthwhile for those of your products that are already clearly differentiated from competing products. Identify which of your products are highly differentiated, and analyze them first. As you work your way back toward the least differentiated products, it will eventually become apparent that the analysis is no longer resulting in any profit improvements on your remaining products, so you can halt the analysis at this point.

## The Dissipation of Value Over Time

When you are providing services to correct a major issue for a customer, the customer is likely to consider the value of this service to be quite high – right up until the moment when you correct the issue that the customer is experiencing. From that point onward, the customer's pain level associated with the issue plummets, which will make it much more difficult to collect a robust fee from the customer. This is why so many attorneys charge their clients a retainer before agreeing to represent them (especially when criminal charges have been filed). Here are several examples of the dissipation of value that cover activities other than legal services:

- Repairing a broken air conditioner in the summer.
- Repairing a broken furnace in the winter.
- Repairing a broken water heater just before visitors arrive.
- Test preparation tutoring prior to taking college entrance examinations.
- IT support when a key computer system is not functioning.
- Data recovery services when a computer system fails.

In all of the preceding cases, it would make a great deal of sense to obtain payment in advance, while the customer's perception of value is high.

## Value Pricing Sales Techniques

It can be difficult to convince a customer that your product provides sufficient incremental value over competing offerings to be worth a higher price point. Here are some ways to convince the customer:

- *Offer a free trial.* Give the customer some time to use the product for free, and arrive at its own conclusion regarding product value. A bonus would be to offer free support to the customer during this service, in order to assist in identifying the key value-creating features.
- *Offer a rebate if the value does not materialize.* This can be a difficult option, since you may end up arguing with the customer over how it quantifies the value of your product.

- *Offer to share the risk.* Enter into an arrangement where you split the quantified gains from the customer's use of your product. This would require a very specific arrangement that states exactly how the gains would be calculated.
- *Add ancillary products.* Customers may be more inclined to pay a higher price if you add a package of ancillary products to what they are buying. For example, you could add a training session, or an instruction manual, or a repair kit – or all three. These items may be relatively inexpensive to provide, and yet are perceived by customers to have real value.

**Tip:** Consider adding an unidentified gift to each order. This provides some level of value to the customer, while allowing you to give away some slow-moving inventory or inventory that was relatively inexpensive.

## Transactional Pricing Adjustments

There are a number of easy analyses that can reveal, on a customer-by-customer basis, where there are opportunities for pricing adjustments. Here are some options to consider:

- *Adjust pricing to emphasize the best product mix.* If you have a mix of products that generates the highest possible profit, then alter your pricing to make this mix more appealing to customers. If the most profitable mix varies by region (perhaps due to shipping costs), then adjust the pricing to maximize profits at a regional level.
- *Alter packaging discounts.* Periodically examine your discount structure for package sizes, so that your prices are higher for smaller package quantities.
- *Alter volume discounts.* Increase the volumes that customers must attain before they will be granted volume discounts. You might adjust this volume figure annually, perhaps to concentrate discounts with only the largest 10% or 20% of customers.
- *Eliminate pricing term variances.* Identify those customers that are receiving long payment terms, and develop a plan to revise those terms back toward your standard terms. This can be difficult, since your largest customers are likely the ones that have negotiated these favorable deals.
- *Impose minimum order quantities.* Does it make sense to impose a minimum order quantity on customers? By doing so, you may be able to reduce your shipping costs.
- *Investigate servicing fees.* If you are providing services along with your products, investigate whether you are charging enough for them. For example, you may be providing installation services or ongoing maintenance for which customers are locked in to your services group.
- *Look for price spreads.* Run an analysis that compares your target prices to the prices actually being charged to customers. If any customers are being billed inordinately low prices, then consider whether you can raise their prices

to a point closer to your target prices. This may be a multi-year effort, to gradually accustom these customers to higher prices.

- *Research late payments.* See if any customers consistently pay late, and develop a plan to start charging them late fees whenever this happens.
- *Review customization deals.* If customers are asking for product customizations (such as special features or packaging), investigate whether you can raise the prices charged for these services.
- *Shift sales to the most profitable distribution channel.* Conduct a profit analysis for each of your distribution channels, and take steps to shift more customers into those channels that generate the most profit.

**Charge for Free Services**

A variation on the theme of raising prices is to charge for services that are currently free. This can include the following:

- *Rush fee.* If a customer wants delivery sooner than the promised date, add a substantial additional charge, and increase the fee further for overnight delivery.
- *Fuel surcharges.* The cost of energy is always increasing, so why not pass it along to customers in the form of a fuel surcharge?
- *Credit card fee.* These fees usually start at 3% of a transaction's price and go up from there, and so can be a significant burden on the profits of a seller. However, adding a surcharge to a purchase transaction is commonly viewed in a negative manner by customers, since it is essentially a penalty for using a credit card. A reasonable way to deal with the situation is to raise list prices enough to cover the cost of credit card fees, and then offer a discount for cash payments.
- *Shipping and handling fees.* Unless there is competition in the industry based on free delivery, be sure to charge a reasonable amount for shipping and handling. Do not overcharge in this area – the prevalence of free shipping in some areas has made consumers more sensitive to this type of fee.

An area particularly worthy of a fee is rapid order deliveries. Compile the cost of accelerated deliveries (such as overnight or two-day deliveries) and determine the incremental difference in cost compared to a normal delivery. If this difference is significant, and especially if this is not a differentiating service feature for your business, then charge extra for it.

Another possibility is to experiment with increasing prices for new product features. If customers are willing to pay a higher price for these features, then you are providing something that they want. If they are not willing to pay a higher price, then you have probably invested in new product features that customers do not care about. In the latter case, considered scaling back the unwanted new feature in order to save money, and shift the funds into some other feature for which customers *are* willing to pay more (see the Target Costing chapter for more information).

## Price Increase Experimentation

When engaging in price increases, do so on an experimental basis. This means setting up a pricing experiment to measure how unit sales decrease in response to a price increase. If there is a net increase in overall profitability despite a decline in unit sales, then broadly roll out the price increase. Conversely, if there is a sharp decline in unit volume during an experimental price increase, then terminate the experiment and return the price to its original level.

---

**Tip:** When you conduct a price increase experiment, do not immediately roll it back if you receive pushback from customers. In some cases, customers may take their business elsewhere, but then return after they realize that other options in the marketplace are worse. Only by sticking with a price increase for a modest period of time can you determine how many customers were serious about their unhappiness with the new prices.

---

It is essential to have a robust feedback loop from the sales staff whenever you are experimenting with a price increase. They can tell you about customer responses to the increase, as well as how well any associated marketing materials worked. This information can then be used to adjust either the price or the marketing materials as part of the ongoing experiment.

---

**Tip:** Consider experimenting with prices in your lowest-profit market segments. If the price increase succeeds, then you have just improved the financial health of this segment. If the price increase fails, there is no real downside, since you might have been considering shutting down this segment anyways (as described further in the next section).

---

## Eliminate Unprofitable Customers

Some of your customers are probably unprofitable. They demand unusually low prices, or take an inordinate number of discounts, or send back an unconscionable number of products. They may also hog the time of your customer service staff. The following grid is useful for categorizing customers by profit and volume level. Ideally, you should minimize sales to those customers in the lower left corner of the grid, and work to push all other customers into the high-volume high-profit quadrant in the upper right corner of the grid.

**Customer Profitability Grid**

| High Volume - Low Profit | High Volume - High Profit |
|---|---|
| Avian Supply | Highway Presentations |
| Beatrice Acquisitions | Illustrious Cleaners |
| Carroll Manufacturing | Jingo Products |
| Dork Designs | Killer Company |
| Enough Supply | Lingo Linguistics |
| Franklin Marbles | Morton Sugar |
| Gorilla Suit Rentals | Nana Supply Company |
| **Low Volume - Low Profit** | **Low Volume - High Profit** |
| Ortho Products | Verity Copy Review |
| Pippa Plumbing | Wilson Tires |
| Quandary Location Services | Xenon Lighting |
| Rudolph Delivery Service | Yampa Culinary |
| Stevens Legal Services | Zorro Fencing Tutelage |
| Torrent Gutter Cleaning | Arbor Tree Pruning |
| Unbelievable Delivery | Boris Private Eye |

The customers on the left (low profit) side of the grid represent an excellent source of future profits, which can be achieved using either of the following alternatives:

- Notify selected unprofitable customers that you will no longer be doing business with them (thereby eliminating their associated losses).
- Raise prices to your remaining unprofitable or low-profit customers to a sufficient extent that you will subsequently earn a reasonable profit from them.

It is entirely possible that raising the prices charged to these customers will lead to them taking their business elsewhere, which is essentially a win for your business.

**Note:** Do not take either of the preceding steps if you do not have a clear understanding of the losses you are currently incurring from sales to your worst customers. This means developing a report that itemizes the gross sales from all of your customers, minus the discounts, returns, bad debt losses, and additional staffing costs associated with each one. Be sure to include the interest cost of any unusually long credit terms granted to customers, as well. Only with this much hard information can you fully understand the extent of the losses being incurred.

An added advantage of eliminating your least profitable customers is that this opens up more of your production capacity, which can now be used to service new customers who are willing to pay your prices. This may result in a great deal of excess capacity, if you have decided to lose a large customer that generated a significant part of your sales (such as a large retail chain).

---

**EXAMPLE**

Big Retailer places an order for 100,000 widgets from Puny Corp., but demands a special price of just $9 per unit, which is less than its standard price of $12 per unit. In addition, it demands 120-day payment terms. The cost per unit for Puny is $8, and the cost of its line of credit is 10%.

Initially, it appears that Puny will earn a profit of $1 on each unit sold, for a total of $100,000. However, Big Retailer is not paying for 90 days longer than Puny's other customers. This means that Puny is supporting the $800,000 cost of the units sold for a quarter of a year, which represents $20,000 of extra financing costs, but still yields a profit of $80,000. So far, it makes sense to stick with Big Retailer.

However, after a few months, Puny realizes that Big is returning thousands of unsold widgets that were damaged in its warehouse. Puny cannot repair or resell these units, and has to write them off as a loss – which comes to $90,000. Overall, this means that Puny has incurred a $10,000 loss on the Big Retailer purchase order. Puny's managers could attempt to negotiate a price hike with Big, but decide that the overall experience has been so poor that it makes more sense to drop the customer entirely.

---

A further advantage of losing your lowest-profit customers is that they are probably your most price-sensitive ones, and so are most likely to complain about any price increase that you want to enact. By allowing these customers to go away due to a price increase, you are eliminating a pain point in running your business. Since most people prefer to avoid negative customer interactions, this means that subsequent price increases should be easier for you.

A concern sometimes put forward when discussing dropping customers is that this will negatively impact your market share. This is an entity's proportion of the total sales generated within the applicable market. Business schools routinely point out that increasing market share is a great way to deny sales to competitors, and build your production volumes in order to drive down your costs. The problem with this logic is that any market is comprised of customers from whom a profit can be extracted, and those who inevitably cause you to incur losses. The trick is to only expand market share up to the point where you are servicing profitable customers. You should be gleefully shifting all other customers onto the competition, who will have an abysmal time trying to squeeze any profits out of the situation – no matter how big their market share may be.

---

**EXAMPLE**

Owl Corporation currently has 10,000 profitable customers who value its service offerings. The firm earns $8 million in profits every year. Its management team wants to see if it can expand its market share by 20%, and hires a consultant to advise them on how to do so. The consultant points out that everyone left in the market has a lower income than the firm's current customer base, and so will require ongoing discounts in order to buy from Owl. In addition, and because of their lower incomes, management should expect the bad debt percentage to triple, which will also require the hiring of two more bad debt collectors. In addition, the company will need to invest an additional $2 million in inventory in order to support the additional sales.

The consultant quantifies these issues, and concludes that the company will earn an additional $500,000 by expanding its market share into this next tranche of customers. After due deliberation, the management team concludes that it is too much trouble to access this additional tranche of customers, especially given the low profit payback, and does not attempt to expand further.

---

The preceding example seems to imply that there is an optimum sales level, beyond which a business should not attempt to expand. This is not really the case. It is also possible to investigate the existing customer base to see if they have any unmet needs, and then do a better job of fulfilling those needs – at an appropriate price point, of course. Expanding the offerings to existing customers tends to build an extremely loyal customer base, which means that the customer turnover level is quite low.

Another option is to expand the current offerings to the same types of customers in other geographic markets that the firm is not currently addressing. This is not so easy, for the following reasons:

- You will need to pay to acquire an entirely new cluster of customers.
- You may need to invest in new infrastructure, such as local warehouses and sales offices.
- There may be competitors already in these markets from which you will have to pry customers.

This does not mean that you should *not* pursue a geographical expansion – only that you should be aware of the additional costs of doing so.

A further consideration is the impact on your infrastructure of eliminating your worst customers. When this happens, you will need fewer support staff, less building space, less inventory, and less production capacity – all while at the same time generating more profits, since you have stripped away those customers who were generating losses. Is that a bad thing? In essence, you are paring back your market share in order to focus on your prime customers, and now require fewer assets to service them. This does not appear to be a bad thing, as long as you can sidestep the presumed loss in prestige of having less market share. Conversely, consider the situation of a competitor who has gleefully picked up your worst customers. This company now has to add staff and invest in more inventory and production equipment in order to service customers who will never generate a profit. When you look at it from this perspective, reducing your market share looks like a good way to not only improve your organization's profits, but also to put your competitors in a worse financial situation.

## Product Line Pricing

It is quite common for a business to set up a product line, which starts with a low-priced version of a product and moves up through several versions to the most deluxe model, replete with advanced features. The price increases for each upgrade in the product line. The theory behind this approach is that customers can segment themselves based on what they need and how much they are willing to spend – the seller is merely providing them with choices. Customers view this type of price segmentation as fair, since the price is not being imposed by the company. For example, a bicycle company offers a basic commuter bike for $300, the same model with full suspension for $600, with a carbon fiber frame for $1,600, and a fully tricked-out mountain bike version with titanium parts for $4,000. Consumers can figure out for themselves which bike fits their needs and their pocketbooks. This good-better-best product differentiation can be described in company marketing materials, so that customers can clearly see the differences. This differentiation can address such matters as the service level provided, the speed or capacity of the product, the level of customer support provided, and the breadth of the associated product warranty.

This approach is also useful from the perspective of your sales staff, since customers will self-select what they want to buy. If they decide to purchase a lower-end product, then you can even direct them to make an online purchase, thereby shifting these customers away from your sales staff. Doing so keeps them from wasting the time of your salespeople, who will be more interested in selling higher-priced products that have more profits associated with them. An added benefit of only selling cheaper products online is that people buying these goods are more intently focused on price, and so would otherwise be more likely to waste the time of the sales staff, trying to bargaining down the price.

## The Use of Bundling

A business can alter its total revenue by clustering several goods and services together into a single package price (called *bundling*). When structured properly, bundling can be used to increase profits, for the following reasons:

- It can pair a low-price primary purchase (such as a television) with a higher-margin add-on (such as a warranty for that television).
- It increases your overall sales volume. Even when your margins are generally relatively low, the use of bundling will increase the overall margin generated.
- Since your sales are increasing, this implies that customers are purchasing more from you and less from the competition. In effect, this is a competitive blocking move.
- It implies that the price is not negotiable, since you have already included a modest discount in the standard price of the bundle.

- It requires minimal extra sales effort. Asking if someone wants to buy an installation service or a training plan is the work of a few moments, and so tends to generate significant additional sales per extra minute of sales time invested.
- It reduces the total administrative effort. It takes less time to record a bundled sale in the accounting records than it does to record each individual item separately. If there are many bundled sales, this could save you the cost of an accountant.
- It represents a point of differentiation from those of your competitors who are not offering bundled products.

> **Tip:** When formulating what goes into a bundle, always calculate your profit for each combination of goods and services. Ideally, a bundle should provide a combination of great perceived value for the customer and the highest possible profit for you.

In addition, customers are more likely to purchase bundles, since a single bundle purchase is an easier decision than working through a menu of choices and deciding which mix of individual products or services to acquire.

The bundling concept can be used to segment your customers into those that are price-sensitive and those that are not. For example, a gold-level medical insurance plan offers customers very low deductibles in exchange for a higher up-front price, while a bronze-level insurance plan offers customers much higher deductibles in exchange for a lower up-front price. The price-sensitive customers will routinely pick the bronze plan, while wealthier (and presumably less price-sensitive) customers will probably pick the gold plan. Setting up a range of these bundles at different price points is also a good way to maximize your profits, since you can tailor solutions for each level of customer. Otherwise, if you were to offer just one bundle to all of your customers, only a portion of them would consider the offer to be a good value – the other customers might be more inclined to take their business elsewhere, to a competitor that offers a broader range of bundle options.

**EXAMPLE**

Chimney Sweeps Corporation sells a basic annual fireplace cleaning service that costs $150, and includes scrubbing the base of the fireplace and inspecting the gas log for maintenance issues. This service appeals to 50% of its customers, which are price-conscious. It also offers a $250 cleaning service that includes a power scrub of the entire chimney interior, and which minimizes the risk of any chimney fires. This service appeals to the 30% of the company's customers who are risk averse. Finally, it offers a $400 annual cleaning service that includes the previous services, plus a guarantee to replace all failed gas log parts for free. This bundle appeals to the 20% of its customers who are wealthier, who do not want to be bothered with a number of separate servicing bills from Chimney Sweeps. By offering these three services, the company has effectively appealed to the needs of its entire customer base, and captured the maximum amount of profit from them.

If you offer a set of bundled products that are on a pricing continuum (such as $100 for a bronze bundle, $200 for a silver bundle, and $300 for a gold bundle), there are several ways to enhance your prices. Consider the following options:

- *Increase the price of the bottom-most bundle.* Doing so reduces the pricing separation to the next-highest option, and may convince a few price-conscious buyers to switch up to the next-highest option. This concept can only be taken so far, since the most price-conscious customers might leave.
- *Reduce the prices of the higher options.* Doing so may attract more price-conscious customers, while still retaining the most price-conscious at the lowest bundle price point.
- *Establish a very high-priced option.* By adding a very high-priced option to your mix of bundles, the other bundles will seem cheaper by comparison. The result may be few sales of the high-priced option, but more sales of the higher-priced options.
- *Narrow the price gap between the top options.* When there is only a modest pricing difference between your highest-priced options, it is an easier decision for customers to make the jump to the higher-priced offerings – which increases your profit.
- *Experiment with the price of each product.* Ongoing experiments can establish the price that will attract the most customers for each bundle, which may be higher or lower than its current price. Significant changes in price may require you to alter the mix of products being offered, so that customers perceive a fair amount of value for the price being offered.
- *Add cheap extras to the highest-profit bundle.* If one bundle is clearly the most profitable one for you, then consider loading it up with low-cost extras in order to attract the attention of more customers. This is especially useful when there is a distinct profit difference between the bundles.

It may require ongoing experimentation to arrive at the perfect set of contents for each bundle, combined with just the right price that represents good value for the customer and great profits for you. Consider revisiting these components on a regular basis to see if you are still operating in this "sweet spot."

## Offer Options

What about a situation in which you are having difficulty closing sales at a reasonable price point? For example, a customer wants to buys an extremely high-end Italian sofa, but your price point is out of reach for her. Is this the time to regretfully escort your prospective customer out the door, thereby losing the sale forever? Not necessarily. You may still be able to secure the sale by spending a bit more time with her to more fully understand what this person feels is important. Here are some areas of concern that might be of interest to the customer:

- Being able to delay payment for a few months
- Being able to add a footstool to the purchase for a reduced price

- Having the sofa shipped directly to her home from the factory on an expedited basis
- Having a few of your movers deliver it and spend some extra time shifting around her other furniture to make room for the sofa
- Having her specify a unique fabric to be used in the construction of the sofa

If you find that one of these options is of exceptional value to the customer, you might still be able to close the deal without impinging too much on your targeted profit margin. For example, one of the preceding options was to add a footstool to the purchase for a reduced price; if you know that the footstool already has an unusually high margin, then adding it to the order at a discount will still be a good deal for you. In short, engaging with customers to learn more about their situations can result in a more tailored solution that can still secure a profitable sale. The only real risk to this approach is that your sales staff will have to invest more time in each customer, which may or may not result in a sale.

## Discount Avoidance

The most common practice employed by businesses to secure a sale is to offer a discount. The problem with this approach is that the amount of the discount falls straight through to the bottom line. For example, a 20% discount on a $100 list price means that your before-tax profit just dropped by $20. If the product being sold is relatively low margin, this discount might have wiped out or at least significantly reduced the amount earned.

---

**EXAMPLE**

Runner's Delight is a shoe store that sells both road running and trail running shoes. Its current gross margin is 40%. Its owner is trying to drum up new business, and so offers a 10% discount to every customer coming into its store. Since everyone is taking the discount, this reduces the store's gross margin to 30%, making it more difficult to pay its operating costs. After a few months, the owner realizes that 95% of the discounts are being taken by existing customers who would have bought the shoes anyways whenever their old shoes wore out. In effect, he was cutting profits by 25% in order to attract 1/20th of the company's total customer base.

---

Are there better alternatives to a discount that have a lesser impact on your bottom line? Here are some options:

- *Add a free product to the sale.* If you have some excess inventory, then adding it to a customer's purchase is an easy way to provide value – and by eliminating inventory that was taking up excess space in your warehouse.
- *Add a free warranty.* Most customers never make a warranty claim, so offering one is – in most cases – free, while still providing the customer with some perceived value.

- *Add free telephone support*. Many customers never need any support services, so offering it for free may not place much of an incremental burden on your support staff.
- *Invest more sales time*. Encourage your sales staff to spend more time talking to clients, explaining all of a product's features. This does use up valuable sales time, but may build a strong case with customers for why you are not going to offer them a discount.

In short, consider all possible alternatives before offering a discount. And if you absolutely must do so, then make it the exception, not an ongoing occurrence. Furthermore, put a hard cap on the amount of discounts granted, with the intent of gradually reducing the amount over time. Eventually, these actions should add up to substantial profit gains.

> **Tip:** A good way to emphasize the financial impact of discounts with management is to produce a monthly report that shows the gross amount of discounts granted to customers, along with a listing of the customers to which these discounts were granted – sorted in descending order by discount volume. This is a good way to spotlight the most egregious discounts being granted.

> **Tip:** It makes great financial sense to impose tight controls over the issuance of discounts to customers, given the impact on profits. To put this in perspective, a business that routinely offers 20% discounts to its customers will likely find that the cost of these discounts is its third-largest expense, after its cost of goods sold and compensation costs. Many businesses impose much stricter controls over expenses that have a far smaller impact on their profits.

> **Tip:** Track discounts by salesperson. It is quite possible that some salespeople are using discounts much more than others in order to secure sales from customers. It may be necessary to re-educate these people regarding the financial impact of discounts. Or, if they persist in damaging your profits with heavy discounting practices, then impose tight approval controls on them, or fire them.

## Loss Leader Adjustments

Some retailers like to offer a *loss leader*, where they advertise deep discounts on a few items. The underlying premise is that customers will come into their stores to buy these items, and then buy other, regularly-priced items as well. This is a theory that may or may not be correct. For example, a price-conscious customer may come into one of these stores solely to buy the advertised loss leader, and then immediately departs and continues the remainder of his shopping at a different store. An analysis of customer purchases can likely identify whether this is the case. If so, there are several ways to alter a loss leader arrangement in order to still generate a reasonable profit. Here are some options:

- The loss leader price is only available if you also purchase $__ of other items that are not designated discount items. This approach assures you of generating a profit on the other purchases, even if you do not on the discount items.
- The loss leader price is only available if you make $___ of purchases from the store on a monthly basis. This approach reserves the really good deals for the store's best customers, and encourages them to purchase exclusively from the store in order to access the best discount deals.
- The loss leader price is only applied to the third/fourth/fifth unit purchased, where the other units are purchased at full price. This is essentially a volume discount.

## Monitor Market Capacity

Changes in the amount of production capacity in a market can have a significant impact on pricing. When new capacity becomes available, its owner needs to sell in sufficient volume to cover the facility's fixed costs. This creates downward pressure on prices, and so can reduce your profits over the long term.

This is not much of an issue in an expanding market, where new capacity must be installed in order to meet demand. However, it is a much greater concern when the capacity is being added to a flat or declining market. In these cases, you might consider locking customers into longer-term contracts before new capacity is created, in order to maintain profits for as long as possible. Otherwise, the likely outcome will be a gradual profit decline as market prices drop.

An interesting pricing opportunity arises when capacity is removed from a market. This can cause an immediate supply squeeze that will probably trigger a jump in prices. If so, a good pricing play is to avoid long-term supply contracts when you are aware of a looming capacity drop, so that you can immediately take advantage of the supply squeeze and increase your prices.

---

**EXAMPLE**

A single oil refinery services the Denver-area market. Every ten years, it must be shut down for maintenance, which takes six months to complete. During that time, the prices of gasoline, heating oil, and aviation fuel all spike in the Denver area, because of the sudden drop in supply. Once the oil refinery maintenance is completed, prices return to normal.

---

## Other Factors Impacting Your Prices

There are several other factors that can reinforce an emphasis of providing value to customers. They are as follows:

- *Base commissions on profits generated.* If your salespeople are paid a commission that is derived from the revenue dollars they have generated, then they will do whatever it takes to make a sale – including offering price cuts to the customer. This is only rational, since they are being compensated based on the sales dollars generated. However, if you change the commission calculation to be based on the profits generated, then they will work much harder to ensure that all sales generated are profitable ones – otherwise, their commissions will decline.

- *Fire salespeople who focus on price.* If you have salespeople who always try to gain sales by cutting prices, then firing them may be the most efficient action to take. Rather than attempting to re-train them, search for replacement salespeople whose natural inclination is to provide increased value at a higher price.
- *Set floor prices for sales staff.* It is essential to set a hard floor for the prices to which salespeople can discount from your list price. Any prices below that floor must be approved by the sales manager or someone in senior management. This is especially important when the sales staff routinely cuts prices in order to secure sales. Also, by shifting the discount-granting decision to a supervisor who is (presumably) not in front of the customer, the salesperson can blame the tight-fisted supervisor for not granting the requested discount.
- *Conduct value sales training.* The sales staff will need ongoing training in communicating product value to customers, in order to support price increases. This is a particular concern when they have previously been compensated for offering discounts, since they may have a hard time adjusting to the new sales strategy.

## Install Proper Price Administration

To maximize profits, you must have an adequate administrative back-end to your pricing methodology to ensure that the prices being set are actually charged to customers. This means posting new prices on the agreed-upon dates, with proper notice to customers, as well as ensuring that these new prices are immediately included in customer billings as of their effective date. Price administration also involves auditing customer billings to ensure that the amounts billed to them match what was agreed upon in the underlying contracts. Without these admittedly boring activities being conducted with great precision, it is quite likely that your business will experience some profit leakage.

---

**Tip:** As you go through a series of price increases over time, track the amount of time it takes to complete each pricing update. If this requires significant negotiations with customers, then it may require a number of months to complete. The longer it takes to implement a price increase, the lower your profits will be in the meantime. A good ongoing best practice is to keep track of which issues delayed the latest price rollout, and work on minimizing these issues the next time around. Over time, you should be able to reduce the implementation period, thereby increasing your profits.

---

## How to Reduce Prices

There may be times when the situation calls for a price decrease, perhaps because you will otherwise lose a major customer, or because worsening economic conditions demand it. This may be especially necessary when a major competitor will take over the account, or when your value proposition is declining in relation to the offerings of competitors. When this happens, there are several ways to minimize the damage to your profits. Consider the following options:

- *Gain a concession in exchange.* If you have to reduce your price, then look for an offset. For example, shorten the customer's payment terms, or stop providing the customer with free shipping, or ask for a longer contract commitment. Other options are to remove the product warranty, take away the free training session, or have the customer pay for any customer service calls.
- *Delay the price implementation.* Every day at the current price point maintains your existing profit margin, so delay the new price for as long as possible.
- *Minimize the reduction.* There are many options for minimizing the amount of a reduction. This might involve a discount that is only in effect for a specific period of time, after which the price returns to its previous level. Another option is to only reduce the price on the customer's last increment of purchases. For example, the first 1,000 units are priced at $10.00, while everything over that quantity is priced at $8.00. Another option is to take away the customer's volume discounts in exchange for the price reduction. As another possibility, offer a price reduction on a replacement product for which you earn a larger margin.

---

**Tip:** Try to avoid a price reduction when it will be visible to your other customers, since they will likely demand a price reduction, too.

---

## The Frequency of Pricing Discussions

A good pricing best practice is simply to continually re-address the pricing topic on a regular basis. Most organizations only review their prices once a year, and even then may only address the topic in terms of modest changes from whatever was charged in the previous year. Instead, and given the massive impact of price changes on your bottom line, pricing should actually be designated as one of the most critical, ongoing management topics. This means that it should be brought up continually, to ensure that prices are being set at levels that maximize your profits. Better yet, if your business is large enough to support it, have at least one full-time person (if not an entire team) constantly researching every aspect of your prices, those of your competitors, and the value being generated for customers to see if there are any pricing adjustments to be made.

More frequent pricing discussions is also a good way to adjust pricing to your organization's capacity constraints, staffing, and inventory issues, as well as external market issues, which may fluctuate significantly within a year. For example, if a competitor goes out of business, this may crimp supply in the market, allowing you to immediately raise prices. Or, the release of a new product version might mandate discounting your old products in order to remove them from inventory before they become obsolete.

> **Tip:** Conducting a pricing analysis on a regular basis sharpens your pricing skills, since it leads to the development of pricing analysis templates and procedures, as well as more in-house expertise.

## Summary

The single most important issue covered in this chapter was that profit maximization involves targeting the profitable sectors of the market, and not attempting to pursue the rest of it. If you try to increase your market share, you will soon find that this can only be done by pursuing tranches of increasingly price-sensitive customers. You may indeed increase your market share, but only by reducing your prices. The result may very well be more revenue, but less profit. In short, be extremely disciplined about the prices you are willing to charge, and leave the least profitable segments of the market to others.

# Chapter 2
# Constraint-Based Pricing

## Introduction

The prices of products and services are usually set by the sales and marketing department, which may use a number of pricing methodologies to determine prices. These methodologies rarely take account of the presence of a constraint, which can lead to adverse price points that do not optimize profits. In this chapter, we give an overview of the different types of pricing strategies, and then move to a discussion of how constraint-based pricing is formulated and employed.

## Pricing Strategies

There are a number of pricing strategies that a company can use. In this section, we aggregate the many strategies into categories and briefly describe each one. The alternatives noted in this section can then be compared to the constraint-based pricing concept noted in the following sections.

### Cost-Based Pricing Strategies

These pricing strategies are based on the cost of the underlying product or service. They are:

- *Absorption pricing*. Includes all variable costs, as well as an allocation of fixed costs. It may include a profit markup. The intent is to ensure that prices are set that will ensure a long-term profit.
- *Break even pricing*. Includes all variable costs, as well as an allocation of fixed costs. It may include a profit markup. The intent is to find that price point at which a business earns a profit of zero.
- *Cost plus pricing*. Includes all variable costs, an allocation of fixed costs, and a predetermined markup percentage. This approach is frequently used in government contracts.
- *Marginal cost pricing*. Prices are set near the marginal cost required to produce an item, usually to take advantage of otherwise-unused production capacity. This method is used to develop prices for special deals.
- *Time and materials pricing*. Customers are billed for the labor and materials incurred by the company, with a profit markup. This method is commonly used for construction projects.

## Value Pricing Strategies

These pricing strategies do not rely upon cost, but rather the perception of customers of the value of the product or service. They are:

- *Dynamic pricing*. Technology is used to alter prices continuously, based on the willingness of customers to pay. This is a common pricing strategy in the airline industry.
- *Premium pricing*. The practice of setting prices higher than the market rate in order to create an aura of exclusivity. This is used by sellers of high-end consumer goods.
- *Price skimming*. The practice of initially setting prices high to reap unusually high profits when a product is initially introduced. This is used by first-to-market innovators.
- *Value pricing*. Prices are set based on the perceived value of the product or service to the customer. This tends to be used for higher-value services, such as investment banking.

## Teaser Pricing Strategies

These strategies are based on the concept of luring in customers with a few low-priced or free products or services, and then cross-selling them higher-priced items. They are:

- *Freemium pricing*. The practice of offering a basic service for free, and charging a price for a higher service level. Commonly used by Internet web sites.
- *High-low pricing*. The practice of pricing a few products below the market rate to bring in customers, and pricing all other items above the market rate. Used by retailers.
- *Loss leader pricing*. The practice of offering special deals on a few items, in hopes of drawing in customers to buy other, regularly-priced items. Used by retailers.

## Strategic Pricing

These strategies involve the use of product pricing to position a company within a market or to exclude competitors from it. They are:

- *Limit pricing*. The practice of setting an unusually low, long-term price that will deter potential competitors from entering a market.
- *Penetration pricing*. The practice of setting a price below the market rate in order to increase market share.
- *Predatory pricing*. The practice of setting prices low enough to drive competitors from the market.
- *Price leadership*. When one company sets a price point that is adopted by competitors. This company is usually the one having the greatest market share.

In short, four broad types of pricing have developed over the years. The first two types, cost-based and value pricing, are the most common. Teaser pricing and strategic pricing are less frequently used. None of these pricing methods take into account the presence of a constraint within a business, even though constraint management is essential to maximizing profits. We will develop the constraint-based pricing concept through the remainder of this chapter.

## Constraint Analysis Financial Terminology

Before we delve into the concept of constraint-based pricing, we need to define several terms that will be used later in this chapter. They are as follows:

- *Throughput*. This is the margin left after totally variable costs are subtracted from revenue. This tends to be a large proportion of revenues, since all overhead costs are excluded from the calculation.
- *Totally variable costs*. This is usually just the cost of materials, since it is only those costs that vary when one incremental unit of a product is manufactured. This does not normally include the cost of labor, since employees are not usually paid based on one incremental unit of output. There are a few other possible costs that may be totally variable, such as commissions, subcontractor fees, customs duties, and freight costs.
- *Operating expenses*. This is all company expenses other than totally variable costs. There is no differentiation between overhead costs, administrative costs or financing costs – quite simply, *all* other company expenses are lumped into this category.
- *Investment*. This is the amount invested in assets. The term includes changes in the level of working capital resulting from a management decision.
- *Net profit*. This is throughput, less operating expenses.

## Constraint Analysis from a Financial Perspective

When a company is examined from the perspective of constraints, it no longer makes sense to evaluate individual products, because overhead costs do not vary at the individual product level. In reality, most companies spend a great deal of money to maintain a production infrastructure, and that infrastructure is what really generates a profit – the trick is making that infrastructure produce the maximum profit with the best mix of products having the highest possible throughput. Under the constraint analysis model, there are three ways to improve the financial position of the entire production infrastructure. They are:

- *Increase throughput*. This is by either increasing revenues or reducing the amount of totally variable costs.
- *Reduce operating expenses*. This is by reducing some element of overhead expenses.

- *Improve the return on investment.* This is by either improving profits in conjunction with the lowest possible investment, or by reducing profits slightly along with a correspondingly larger decline in investment.

Note that only the increase in throughput is related in any way to decisions made at the product level. The other two improvement methods may be concerned with changes anywhere in the production system.

These concepts are included in the following three formulas, which are used to solve a number of financial analysis scenarios:

$$\text{Revenue} - \text{totally variable expenses} = \text{throughput}$$

$$\text{Throughput} - \text{operating expenses} = \text{net profit}$$

$$\text{Net profit} \div \text{investment} = \text{return on investment}$$

When altering the system of production, one or more of the preceding formulas can be used to decide whether the contemplated alteration will improve the system. There must be a positive answer to one of the following questions, or else no action should be taken:

- Is there an incremental increase in throughput?
- Is there an incremental reduction in operating expenses?
- Is there an incremental increase in the return on investment?

The best system improvements are those that increase the amount of throughput generated, since there is no theoretical upper boundary on the amount of throughput.

## The Constraint Analysis Model

There is an excellent constraint analysis model that was developed by Thomas Corbett, and which is outlined here. The basic thrust of the model is to give priority in the constraint to those products that generate the highest throughput per minute of constraint time. After these products are manufactured, priority is then given to the product having the next highest throughput per minute, and so on. Eventually, the production queue is filled, and the operation can accept no additional work.

The key element in the model is the use of throughput per minute, because the key limiting factor in a constraint is time – hence, maximizing throughput within the shortest possible time frame is paramount. Note that throughput *per minute* is much more important than total throughput *per unit*. The following example illustrates the point.

**EXAMPLE**

Mole Industries manufactures trench digging equipment. It has two products with different amounts of throughput and processing times at the constrained resource. The key information about these products is:

| Product | Total Throughput | Constraint Processing Time | Throughput per Minute |
|---|---|---|---|
| Mole Hole Digger | $400 | 2 minutes | $200 |
| Mole Driver Deluxe | 800 | 8 minutes | 100 |

Of the two products, the Mole Driver Deluxe creates the most overall throughput, but the Mole Hole Digger creates more throughput per minute of constraint processing time. To determine which one is more valuable to Mole Industries, consider what would happen if the company had an unlimited order quantity of each product, and could run the constrained resource non-stop, all day (which equates to 1,440 minutes). The operating results would be:

| Product | Throughput per Minute | | Total Processing Time Available | | Total Throughput |
|---|---|---|---|---|---|
| Mole Hole Digger | $200 | × | 1,440 minutes | = | $288,000 |
| Mole Driver Deluxe | 100 | × | 1,440 minutes | = | 144,000 |

Clearly, the Mole Hole Digger, with its higher throughput per minute, is much more valuable to Mole Industries than its Mole Driver Deluxe product. Consequently, the company should push sales of the Mole Hole Digger product whenever possible.

The constraint analysis model is essentially a production plan that itemizes the amount of throughput that can be generated, as well as the total amount of operating expenses and investment. In the sample model, we use four different products, each requiring some processing time in the constraint. The columns in the model are as follows:

- *Throughput per minute.* This is the total amount of throughput that a product generates, divided by the amount of processing time at the constrained resource.
- *Constraint usage.* This is the number of minutes of processing time required by a product at the constrained resource. This figure is the sum total of both the setup time for a job and the actual run time for the job.
- *Units scheduled.* This is the number of units scheduled to be processed at the constrained resource.
- *Total constraint time.* This is the total number of minutes of processing time required by a product, multiplied by the number of units to be processed.
- *Total throughput.* This is the throughput per minute multiplied by the number of units processed at the constrained resource.

This grid produces a total amount of throughput to be generated if production proceeds according to plan. Below the grid of planned production, there is a subtotal of the total amount of throughput, from which the total amount of operating expenses are subtracted to arrive at the amount of profit. Finally, the total amount of investment in assets is divided into the profit to calculate the return on investment. Thus, the model provides a complete analysis of all three ways in which you can improve the results of a company – increase throughput, decrease operating expenses, or increase the return on investment. An example of the model follows.

## Sample Constraint Analysis Model

| Product | Throughput per Minute | Constraint Usage (minutes) | Units Scheduled | Total Constraint Time | Total Throughput |
|---|---|---|---|---|---|
| 1. Hedgehog Deluxe | $80 | 14 | 1,000 | 14,000 | $1,120,000 |
| 2. Hedgehog Mini | 70 | 20 | 500 | 10,000 | 700,000 |
| 3. Hedgehog Classic | 65 | 40 | 200 | 8,000 | 520,000 |
| 4. Hedgehog Digger | 42 | 10 | 688 | 6,880 | 288,960 |
| | | Total constraint scheduled time | | 38,880 | |
| | | Total constraint time available* | | 38,880 | |
| | | | Total throughput | | $2,628,960 |
| | | | Total operating expenses | | 2,400,000 |
| | | | Profit | | $228,960 |
| | | | Profit percentage | | 8.7% |
| | | | Investment | | $23,000,000 |
| | | | Annualized return on investment | | 11.9% |

* Minutes per month = 30 days × 24 hours × 60 minutes × (1 − 0.10 maintenance time)

In the example, the Hedgehog Deluxe product has the largest throughput per minute, and so is scheduled to be the first priority for production. The Hedgehog Digger has the lowest throughput per minute, so it is given last priority in the production schedule. If there is less time available on the constrained resource, the company should reduce the number of the Hedgehog Digger product manufactured in order to maximize overall profits.

In the middle of the model, the "Total constraint scheduled time" row contains the total number of minutes of scheduled production. The row below it, labeled "Total constraint time available," represents the total estimate of time that the constraint should have available for production purposes during the scheduling period. Since the time scheduled and available are identical, this means that the production schedule has completely maximized the availability of the constrained resource.

One calculation anomaly in the model is that the profit percentage is normally calculated as profit divided by revenues. However, since revenues are not included in the model, we instead use profits divided by throughput. Since throughput is less than revenue, we are overstating the profit percentage as compared to the traditional profit percentage calculation.

Use the constraint analysis model in a before-and-after mode, to see what effect a proposed change will have on profitability or the return on investment. If the model improves as a result of a change, then implement the change.

## The Decision to Sell at a Lower Price

A common scenario is for a customer to promise a large order, but only if the company agrees to a substantial price drop. The sales department may favor such deals, because they bolster the company backlog, earn commissions, and increase market share. The trouble is that these deals also elbow out other jobs that may have higher throughput per minute. If so, the special deal drops overall throughput and may lead to a loss. The following example, which uses the basic constraint model as a baseline, illustrates the problem.

---

**EXAMPLE**

Mole Industries has received an offer from a customer to buy 2,000 units of its highly profitable Hedgehog Deluxe, but only if the company reduces the price. The new price will shrink the Deluxe's throughput per minute to $60. The analysis is:

| Product | Throughput per Minute | Constraint Usage (minutes) | Units Scheduled | Total Constraint Time | Total Throughput |
|---|---|---|---|---|---|
| 1. Hedgehog Deluxe | $60 | 14 | 2,000 | 28,000 | $1,680,000 |
| 2. Hedgehog Mini | 70 | 20 | 500 | 10,000 | 700,000 |
| 3. Hedgehog Classic | 65 | 40 | 22 | 880 | 57,200 |
| 4. Hedgehog Digger | 42 | 10 | 0 | 0 | 0 |
| | Total constraint scheduled time | | | 38,880 | |
| | Total constraint time available* | | | 38,880 | |
| | | | | | |
| | Total throughput | | | | $2,437,200 |
| | Total operating expenses | | | | 2,400,000 |
| | Profit | | | | $37,200 |
| | Profit percentage | | | | 1.5% |
| | Investment | | | | $23,000,000 |
| | Annualized return on investment | | | | 1.9% |

* Minutes per month = 30 days × 24 hours × 60 minutes × (1 – 0.10 maintenance time)

The baseline production configuration generated a profit of $228,960, while this new situation creates a profit of only $37,200. The profit decline was caused by a combination of lower throughput per minute for the Hedgehog Deluxe and the increased production capacity assigned to this lower-throughput product, which displaced other, more profitable products. Note that there was no production capacity available at all for the Hedgehog Digger product. Clearly, the company should reject the customer's offer.

---

## Price Modeling

In some industries where orders are partially or fully customized, the sales department may have a detailed, custom-designed pricing template that creates a price based on potentially dozens of variables. These models are needed to ensure that all aspects of the production process are included in the development of a product, so that the seller can assure itself of a reasonable profit.

An inherent flaw in these models is that they charge customers for setup time. Nearly all workstations in a production process have excess capacity, so even a lengthy setup in these locations is essentially free – there is no cost to the company. The only exception is the constraint location, where setups must be minimized in order to increase throughput. Based on these issues, a possible alternative for a company that wants to fine-tune its price models is to remove all costs related to setup times for non-constraint locations, but to charge a stiff price for setup times at the constraint. Doing so more accurately reflects the realities of constraint management, and may allow a company to charge more competitive prices related to jobs that do not require constraint time.

## Pricing for a Lengthy Setup Time

When there is a long setup time at the constraint for a certain product, the production scheduler is faced with a quandary. If she schedules just the customer order as a discrete job, then the constraint incurs a long setup time that reduces total throughput. However, if she schedules a longer job that produces more units, the result will be additional units going into stock that may not be sold for some time, and which will be subject to obsolescence and damage during that time.

One way out of this quandary is to set a special bulk pricing discount for customers. If an attractive price is set for orders of large quantities, the company can benefit from having production runs of sufficient length to offset a long setup time. This will mean that customer orders will be more infrequent, since customers must work through the larger stocks of goods that they have ordered.

## The Decision to Enter into a Long-Term Contract

A customer may sometimes present a company with an offer to take a long-term contract to supply goods or services. On the plus side, such an arrangement provides guaranteed revenue to the seller for an extended period, which could be of value in a market where sales levels are volatile. However, these contracts also typically mandate a lower price point in exchange for the certainty of long-term demand. If a lower price point is required, this will reduce the throughput associated with the contract.

To see if the deal should be accepted, insert the proposed contract price and quantities into the throughput analysis model described earlier. If the throughput per minute for the contract is quite low, the contract will push out more profitable work, resulting in a profit decline. In addition, because the contract is a long-term one, the company is essentially being asked to push down its profits for the foreseeable future in exchange for a stable flow of orders.

Conversely, if the goods and price points in a proposed contract result in a high throughput per minute, the company is locking in a high level of profitability for a long period of time. In this latter case, the contract should certainly be accepted.

## Pricing When There is no Constraint Impact

What about situations in which a product or service does not use the constrained resource at all? In this case, there are several extra issues to consider, which are:

- *Impact on sprint capacity.* A product may not impinge upon the constrained resource, but it could impinge indirectly, by using up a portion of the excess sprint capacity[1] in the workstations upstream from the constrained resource. If so, there may come a time when the inventory buffer[2] is depleted, and the remaining sprint capacity is so minimal that it takes an inordinate amount of time to rebuild the buffer. In this case, the indirect impact on the constrained resource puts the organization at risk of generating a reduced level of throughput. If so, the solution is to de-emphasize sales of the item in question, or to outsource it entirely.

- *Impact on raw materials.* A product may not use any time at the constrained resource, but it requires some of the same raw materials used by other products that do use the constrained resource. If so, it is possible that a constriction in the amount of available raw materials will shift the constraint to the supplier. If this is a possibility, management needs to decide where it wants the constraint – with the supplier or internally. Another alternative is to decide whether the item can be produced using a different raw material, thereby avoiding any impact on the constrained resource.

If neither of the preceding issues is present, consider setting the price at a level that creates sufficient demand to soak up any excess production capacity that is not related to sprint capacity.

---

**EXAMPLE**

Armadillo Security Armor manufactures several types of body armor. Four items made from spun graphite must be cured in the company's baking oven, which is the constrained resource. The baking time depends on the physical size of the parts inserted into it. Two other items are made from plate steel, and so use other machinery within the company that are not related to the sprint capacity situated upstream from the baking oven.

---

[1] Sprint capacity is an excess amount of production capacity located upstream from the constrained resource, possibly in several different workstations. The intent of having sprint capacity is to ensure that any inventory shortages at the constraint can be rapidly refilled.

[2] There will always be flaws in the production process that result in variability in the flow of materials to the constrained resource. This means that there will always be periods when there is no inventory to feed into the constraint, so that the constraint will not be used. This issue is dealt with by building up a buffer of inventory in front of the constraint.

The relevant information is:

| Product Name | Price | | Variable Costs | | Throughput | Constraint Time* | Throughput per Minute |
|---|---|---|---|---|---|---|---|
| Graphite Chest Plate | $250 | - | 160 | = | $90 | 5 | $18 |
| Graphite Leggings | 140 | - | 90 | = | 50 | 2 | 25 |
| Graphite Mitts | 190 | - | 150 | = | 40 | 2 | 20 |
| Graphite Torso Plate | 425 | - | 285 | = | 140 | 5 | 28 |
| Steel Chest Plate | 95 | | 30 | = | 65 | -- | -- |
| Steel Neck Guard | 45 | - | 15 | = | 30 | -- | -- |

* In minutes

Based on the throughput per minute information in the last column of the table, Armadillo should emphasize sales of its graphite torso plate, since this product generates the highest throughput per minute. Another option is to increase the price of the graphite chest plate, so that the product is no longer mired at the bottom (figuratively speaking) of the rankings.

Another consideration is whether these products are ever sold as bundles. If so, the torso plate should be combined with the mitts and leggings as a bundle, while the graphite chest plate should be excluded. In this case, the main point is that the throughput per minute for the graphite chest plate is significantly lower than for the torso plate.

Both of the steel products have no impact on the baking oven, so there is no constraint time analysis upon which to base a price.

## Dealing with a Market Constraint

If there is no constraint anywhere in a business that can interfere with the sale of goods, the constraint is said to be in the marketplace. A good way to discern whether there are really no constraints within the business is to investigate whether an increase in customer orders would not interfere with the firm's on-time delivery percentage, while maintaining a competitive lead time and not forcing the staff to work overtime. If this is the case, there are no internal constraints.

If so, the key pricing decision is whether a reduction in price will generate more sales, and whether the price reduction will still yield a net increase in throughput. An additional consideration is the cost (or even the availability) of additional working capital to support any additional sales. The seller may have to support larger amounts of accounts receivable and on-hand inventory balances if it chooses to reduce its prices, which may place a limitation on the amount of short-term growth that can be supported without accessing additional outside funding.

If working capital turns out to be the constraint that keeps a business from generating additional sales, the focus on new sales should be on any transactions involving cash payments or short credit terms, while transactions involving longer credit terms are given a lower priority or not accepted.

Another option when the constraint is in the marketplace is to compete on lead time. If the firm's constraints have been eliminated to such an extent that it can offer significantly shorter lead times than the competition, then this can be a focus of competition. Offering shorter lead times is effective when customers are demanding faster delivery times, and especially when competitors are not able to match this capability. A key advantage is that the firm can continue offering the same prices, or even increase them for shorter delivery times, which enhances its profits. Of course, if customers are not overly insistent on faster delivery times, there is no reason to focus on this approach.

> **Tip:** If the firm intends to cut delivery times as a competitive measure, correspond with prospective customers to ascertain how this will impact the rush delivery fees that they have been paying to their current suppliers. There is a good chance that these rush fees will be eliminated, which gives them a reason to start ordering from the company.

> **Tip:** When prospective customers are forced to place orders with long lead times, there is a good chance they are over-ordering due to incorrect forecasts. If so, model for them how their orders (and on-hand inventory) are likely to decrease in size if they buy from the company, using its shorter delivery times. This approach may increase the number of customers.

When the constraint is in the marketplace and the company elects to compete based on shorter delivery times, it is essential to only prospect for customers for whom this is a critical issue. This implies that, for maximum efficiency, the sales department should conduct a quick scan of the marketplace to determine which potential customers need faster deliveries. These entities should become the sole focus of their sales activities; all other prospects can be ignored.

> **Tip:** The lower lead time offer should result in an increase in sales. If so, maintain a careful watch over your constraints to see if delivery times start to increase. This will require quick action to deal with the constraints, so that delivery commitments can continue to be made to customers.

Of the two competition options presented here – lowering prices or lowering lead times – which is better? An offer of reduced lead time is the best option, since in many cases the competition has not ground down or worked around its constraints in order to be in a position to make the same offer. They simply cannot match the offer, which gives the company a sustained competitive advantage – and without having to lower its prices. Further, competitors may believe that the company will have to incur additional costs in order to make this reduce lead time offer, and so expect it to eventually give up and go back to the industry-standard lead time; this belief can lead them to not even try to match the firm's lead time offer, resulting in a very sustained advantage.

## Objections to Constraint-Based Pricing

Some objections have been raised to the use of constraint analysis in the derivation of prices. These objections are as follows:

- *Short-term pricing.* If many orders are accepted at low price points, not all expenses will be covered, resulting in losses over the long-term. This is true, if a large proportion of orders are sold at low price points. However, if price points are higher for most orders, and constraint analysis is only used to fill any remaining unused production capacity, it can incrementally increase profits.
- *Equipment changeovers.* The cost of equipment setup is not included in the derivation of throughput-based prices, because these costs are not totally variable. The result could be the waste of a large amount of production time doing equipment changeovers for small orders. This assertion is not true, as long as the changeovers involve equipment for which there is excess production capacity. It is only an issue if the changeovers involve the bottleneck operation, in which case there would indeed be a negative impact on throughput. The result should be a willingness to accept a broader range of order sizes and product mixes, up to the point where the extra changeovers begin to create additional bottlenecks within the production process.
- *Lowest-price guarantee.* If the seller has entered into any contracts with the government that require it to offer the government the lowest price offered to any customer, the sales staff should be mindful of the issue when offering prices to other customers when trying to take orders to fill up remaining production capacity.
- *Premium pricing impact.* A company that uses its marketing function to create an aura of exclusivity would have a hard time selling at any price other than the maximum one used for all of its customers. Otherwise, the lower price points could impact the ability of the company to continue selling at its standard retail prices.

In short, there are some valid concerns involving the use of constraint-based pricing, which can be dealt with as long as the sales and production employees are cognizant of how this pricing method should be used.

## Summary

Much of the discussion in this chapter might lead you to believe that a company using constraint-based pricing is continually cutting deals with customers and altering its prices, perhaps on a daily basis. This is not the case – we are merely discussing what to do when certain pricing situations arise, which will probably be at long intervals. Most of the time, prices are set for standard products, and are not changed. In this latter situation, there is no question about which products have the highest throughput per minute, and the entire sales and marketing function is designed to maximize the sales of these products. Usually, only the introduction or withdrawal of a product will trigger any of the analyses noted in this chapter.

# Chapter 3
# Target Costing

## Introduction

A different view of pricing for profit is to develop products that are specifically designed to generate targeted profit levels. In essence, a business determines its profit in advance, and then works backwards through the product design process to create goods that will generate that profit at specific, pre-planned price points. If it cannot manufacture a product at these planned levels, then it cancels the product. This approach is called *target costing*. With target costing, a management team has a powerful tool for continually monitoring products from the moment they enter the design phase and onward throughout their product life cycles.

This chapter describes how target costing works.

---

**Related Podcast Episode:** Episode 57 of the Accounting Best Practices Podcast discusses target costing. It is available at: **accountingtools.com/podcasts** or **iTunes**

---

## The Basic Steps of Target Costing

Target costing has been in existence for a number of years and is used by many companies, so the primary steps in the process are well defined. They are:

1. *Conduct research.* The first step is to review the marketplace in which the company wants to sell products. The team needs to determine the set of product features that customers are most likely to buy, and the amount they will pay for those features. The team must learn about the perceived value of individual features, in case they later need to determine what impact there will be on the product price if they drop one or more of them. It may be necessary to later drop a product feature if the team decides that it cannot provide the feature while still meeting its target cost. At the end of this process, the team has a good idea of the target price at which it can sell the proposed product with a certain set of features, and how it must alter the price if it drops some features from the product.

2. *Calculate maximum cost.* The company provides the design team with a mandated gross margin that the proposed product must earn. By subtracting the mandated gross margin from the projected product price, the team can easily determine the maximum target cost that the product must achieve before it can be allowed into production.

3. *Engineer the product.* The engineers and procurement personnel on the team now take the leading role in creating the product. The procurement staff are particularly important if the product has a high proportion of purchased parts; they must determine component pricing based on the necessary quality, delivery, and quantity levels expected for the product. They may also be

involved in outsourcing parts, if this results in lower costs. The engineers must design the product to meet the cost target, which will likely include a number of design iterations to see which combination of revised features and design considerations results in the lowest cost.

4. *Ongoing activities*. Once a product design is finalized and approved, the team is reconstituted to include fewer designers and more industrial engineers. The team now enters into a new phase of reducing production costs, which continues for the life of the product. For example, cost reductions may come from waste reductions in production (known as kaizen costing, which is the process of continual cost reduction after a product is being manufactured), or from planned supplier cost reductions. These ongoing cost reductions yield enough additional gross margin for the company to further reduce the price of the product over time, in response to increases in the level of competition. Kaizen costing does not generate the size of cost reductions that can be achieved through initial design changes, but it can have a cumulatively significant impact over time.

---

**EXAMPLE**

SkiPS is a maker of global positioning systems (GPS) for skiers, which they use to log how many vertical feet they ski each day. SkiPS conducts a marketing survey to decide upon the features it needs to include in its next generation of GPS device, and finds that skiers want a device they can strap to their arm or leg, and which does not require recharging during a multi-day vacation.

The survey indicates that skiers are willing to pay no more than $150 for the device, while the first review of costs indicates that it will cost $160 to manufacture. At a mandated gross margin percentage of 40%, this means that the device must attain a target cost of $90 ($150 price × (1 − 40% gross margin). Thus, the design team must reduce costs from $160 to $90.

The team decides that the GPS unit requires no display screen at all, since users can plug the device into a computer to download information. This eliminates the LCD display and one computer chip. It also prolongs the battery life, since the unit no longer has to provide power to the display. The team also finds that a new microprocessor requires less power; given these reduced power requirements, the team can now use a smaller battery.

Finally, the team finds that the high-impact plastic case is over-engineered, and can withstand a hard impact with a much thinner shell. After the team incorporates all of these changes, it has reached the $90 cost target. SkiPS can now market a new device at a price point that allows it to earn a generous gross profit.

---

## Value Engineering Considerations

The product engineering process noted above in step three involves many considerations. Here are examples of ways to reduce the cost of a product in order to meet a target cost:

- *Revise the manufacturing process.* The industrial engineering staff may be called upon to create an entirely new manufacturing process that uses less labor or less expensive machinery. It is entirely possible that multiple processes will be entirely eliminated from the production process. In particular, there may be an opportunity to eliminate various quality reviews from the process if product quality can be ensured by other means.
- *Reduce durability.* It is possible that the preliminary product design incorporates a product durability level that is actually *too* robust, thereby creating an opportunity to carefully decrease the level of product durability in order to cut costs. The typical result of this change is to completely eliminate some types of structural reinforcement from the product, or to at least downgrade to a less durable material in some parts of the product.
- *Reduce product features.* It may turn out to be quite expensive to offer certain features in a product. If so, the team needs to decide if it can delete one or more of these features while accepting a lower projected product price for which the net effect is an improved product margin. This type of value engineering must be carefully weighed against the problem of eliminating so many key features that the product will no longer be attractive to customers.
- *Reduce the number of parts.* It may be possible to simplify the design by using fewer parts, especially if doing so reduces the cost of assembling the final product. However, this concept can be taken too far, especially when many standard parts are replaced by a smaller number of customized (and therefore more expensive) parts.
- *Replace components.* It is possible that slightly different components are available at a substantially reduced cost; if so, the design engineers can modify the product to accommodate the different components. This is an especially common avenue when a product is initially designed to include components that have a high per-unit cost, and which can be replaced with components on which the company already earns significant volume discounts by using them across multiple product lines.
- *Design for easier manufacture.* To avoid time-consuming mistakes in the manufacturing process, consider designing the product so that it can only be assembled in a single way – all other attempts to assemble the product in an incorrect manner will fail. By doing so, there will be fewer product failures or recalls, which reduces the total cost of the product. It may be necessary to *increase* the cost of a product in order to create the optimum design for manufacturing, thereby reducing the total cost of the product over its full life span.
- *Ask suppliers.* Suppliers may have significant insights into how to reduce the costs of the various components they are contributing to the final product

design, particularly in regard to altering material content or changing the manufacturing process. Suppliers may be willing to serve on design teams and contribute their expertise in exchange for being the sole source of selected components.

If the project team finds that it can comfortably meet the target cost without engaging in all of the preceding steps, then it should work through the activity list anyways. By doing so, it can generate sufficient room between the actual and target gross margins that management now has the option to reduce the product price below the target level, which may attract additional sales.

## The Cost Reduction Program

The methods used by the design team are more sophisticated than simply saying, "folks, we need to cut $150 in costs – anyone have any ideas?" Instead, the team uses one of two approaches to more tightly focus its cost reduction efforts:

- *Tied to components.* The design team allocates the cost reduction goal among the various product components. This approach tends to result in incremental cost reductions to the same components that were used in the last iteration of the product. This approach is commonly used when a company is simply trying to refresh an existing product with a new version, and wants to retain the same underlying product structure. The cost reductions achieved through this approach tend to be relatively low, but also result in a high rate of product success, as well as a fairly short design period.
- *Tied to features.* The product team allocates the cost reduction goal among various product features, which focuses attention away from any product designs that may have been inherited from the preceding model. This approach tends to achieve more radical cost reductions (and design changes), but also requires more time to design, and also runs a greater risk of product failure or at least greater warranty costs.

Of the two methods noted here, companies are more likely to use the first approach if they are looking for a routine upgrade to an existing product, and the second approach if they want to achieve a significant cost reduction or break away from the existing design.

## The Milestone Review Process

What if the project team simply cannot meet the target cost? Rather than completing the design process and creating a product with a substandard profit margin, the correct response is to stop the development process and move on to other projects instead. This does not mean that management allows its project teams to struggle on for months or years before finally giving up. Instead, they must come within a set percentage of the cost target on various milestone dates, with each successive milestone requirement coming closer to the final target cost. Milestones may occur on specific dates, or when key completion steps are reached in the design process, such as at the end of each design iteration.

---

**EXAMPLE**

Milagro Corporation is developing a new espresso machine that only works with its specially-developed strain of coffee bean. Milagro conducts market research and concludes that the product cannot sell for more than $200. At the company's required gross margin of 40%, this means that the target cost of the product is $120. Management sets a maximum design duration of six months, with milestone reviews at one-month intervals. The results of the month-end milestone reviews are:

| Review Date | Cost Goal | Actual Cost Estimate | Actual Cost Variance from Goal | Allowance Variance From Cost Goal |
|---|---|---|---|---|
| Jan. 31 | $120 | $150 | 25% | 30% |
| Feb. 28 | 120 | 143 | 19% | 20% |
| Mar. 31 | 120 | 138 | 15% | 15% |
| Apr. 30 | 120 | 134 | 12% | 10% |
| May 31 | 120 | Cancelled | -- | 5% |
| June 30 | 120 | Cancelled | -- | 0% |

As the table reveals, the Milagro project team was able to stay ahead of the cost target at the end of the first two months, but then was barely able to meet the allowable variance in the third month, and finally fell behind in the fourth month. Management then cancelled the project, saving itself the cost of continuing the project team for several more months when it was becoming obvious that the team would not be able to achieve the target cost.

---

Though management may cancel a design project that cannot meet its cost goals, this does not mean that the project will be permanently shelved. Far from it. Instead, management should review old projects at least once a year to see if the circumstances have changed sufficiently for them to possibly become viable again. A more precise review approach is to have each project team formulate a set of variables that should initiate a product review if a trigger point is reached (such as a decline in the price of a commodity that is used in the product design). If any of these trigger points are reached, the projects are immediately brought to the attention of management to see if they should be revived.

## Problems with Target Costing

Target costing is difficult to initiate, because of the uncertainty surrounding the eventual release of a product. A company that allows its engineering department sole responsibility for creating products will achieve product releases on a fairly consistent schedule, even though some of the products may not be overly profitable. Under target costing, it is quite possible that a company may cancel a series of projects before they reach fruition, resulting in a frantic marketing department that sees no new products entering the pipeline. The solution is a combination of firm support by senior management and ongoing questioning of whether the target gross margin is too high to be achievable. It is entirely possible that an overly enthusiastic management team sets an excessively high gross margin standard for its new target costing process, and then sees no products survive the process. Consequently, it may take some time before management understands what gross margin levels will result in a target costing process that can churn out an acceptable number of products.

Another problem with target costing is the unwillingness of management to cancel a project. They do not want to see their investment in a project thrown away, and so they keep funding it for "just one more month," hoping that the team will find a way to achieve the target cost. The end result is a very long design process that absorbs more design costs than expected, and which still does not achieve the target cost. The only way to resolve this issue is an iron resolve to terminate projects in a timely manner.

Finally, a design team needs a strong leader to keep control of the opinions of the various departments that are represented on the team. For example, the marketing department may hold out for certain product features, while the design engineers claim that those same features introduce too many costs into the product. The best team leader is not one who unilaterally decides on the product direction, but rather one who can craft a group decision, and if necessary, weed out those who are unwilling to work with the rest of the group.

## The Members of a Design Team

The members of the design team are drawn from multiple disciplines, and their contributions are all essential to the success of a product launch. These positions are:

- *Design engineering*. The design engineers play the most prominent role on the team, since they must create a series of product iterations that incorporate the cost reductions needed to achieve the target cost.
- *Industrial engineering*. A significant part of a product's cost arises during the production process, so industrial engineers must become involved in order to give feedback to the design engineers regarding which design elements should be used that require the lowest production costs.
- *Cost accounting*. An accountant should be with the team at all times, constantly compiling the expected cost of a design as it goes through a series of iterations. The accountant also compares the expected cost to the target cost, and communicates the status of the product cost situation to both the team members and management on a periodic basis.
- *Procurement*. The purchasing department is a valuable contributor to the team, since many components will likely be sourced to third parties, and an experienced procurement person can have a significant positive impact on the cost of purchased components.

- *Marketing*. The marketing department is particularly useful during the initial stages of target costing, where it investigates the prices of competing products and conducts polls to determine the value of specific product features.

## The Role of the Accountant in Target Costing

The accountant's role on a design team is to continually compile the projected cost of the product as it moves forward through the design process. She compares this cost to the total target cost, and communicates the variance between the two figures to management, along with qualitative information about where projected costs are expected to decline further, what design changes are most likely to achieve further cost declines, and how these design changes will affect the value proposition of the final product. Management uses this information to periodically monitor the progress of the design project, and to cancel the project if it appears likely that the product cannot be designed within the cost and value parameters of the project.

It may be necessary to purchase new manufacturing equipment to create a new product. If so, the accountant is the best person to create purchase requests for this equipment, since her normal responsibilities include the review of capital expenditure proposals. Also, since she obviously has a working relationship with the accounting department, she is the best intermediary for relaying any accounting questions about capital proposals.

A key part of the accountant's role is to obtain cost information from suppliers, which in turn is predicated on the assumption of a certain amount of purchasing volume, which may not ultimately prove to be correct. If there are significant cost differences at varying purchase volume levels, it may be necessary for the accountant to present several possible product costs, one for each volume level.

---

**EXAMPLE**

Active Exercise Machines is designing a new treadmill for the home exercise market, and is having trouble pricing the laminated rubber conveyor belt. Since Active is creating a treadmill in a non-standard length, the conveyor belt supplier will incur a setup cost, and must spread this cost over the projected number of treadmills to be produced. Since the setup cost is significant, the cost per unit will decline dramatically if Active orders more conveyor belts. The cost is $95 per unit if Active only orders 5,000 belts, and drops to $50 if Active orders 10,000 belts. Since the total cost of the treadmill is projected to be $500, this difference represents 9% of the total cost, which is significant enough to bring to the attention of management. Consequently, the accountant presents management with two projected costs for the treadmill – one at a unit volume of 5,000, and another at a unit volume of 10,000.

---

The accountant's cost information is likely to be vague when the project is initiated, since she is working with general design concepts and rough estimates of production volumes. Consequently, her initial cost reports are likely to be within a range of possible costs, which gradually tighten up as the team generates more precise designs and better sales estimates.

A final task is for the accountant to continue monitoring the cost of the product after its release, and throughout its product life. This is a key role, because management needs to know immediately if the initial cost structure that the design team worked so hard to create is no longer valid, and why the cost has increased.

The tasks ascribed to the accountant as a member of a design team are not minor. For a larger design project, it is entirely possible that she will be released for special duty to the project, so that no other routine tasks will interfere with her work on the team. In a larger company where product design is the lifeblood of the entity, the accountant may find herself permanently assigned to a series of project teams.

## Data Sources for Target Costing

The accountant may have a difficult time obtaining data from which to develop the cost of a new product design. Here are some of the data sources needed for a target costing project:

- *New components*. The design team may be creating entirely new components from scratch, so there is no cost information available. In this case, the accountant needs to locate roughly comparable components and extrapolate from them what the new components might cost, including tooling costs.

- *Materials sourcing*. Some materials that the design team wants to include in a product may be difficult to obtain, or be subject to significant price swings. The accountant needs to highlight these issues, particularly by using outside sources of historical commodity prices to note the range of price swings that have occurred in the recent past. It is dangerous to only report to management the current market price of these materials, since management may decide to continue product development when it might otherwise drop the project in the face of large potential cost increases.

- *Competitor costs*. It is extremely useful to disassemble competing products to determine what they cost to produce. The accountant can assemble this information into a database, which is useful for not only calculating the likely gross margins that competing products are earning, but also for comparing the design team's choice of components to those used by competitors. In many instances, the design team can copy some aspects of a competing design in order to quickly achieve a lower cost.

- *Production costs*. If a company has engaged in product design for a number of years, it may have developed a table that contains the cost to produce specific components or the cost of the production functions used to create those components. This type of information is difficult to obtain, and requires a great deal of analysis to compile, so having the information available from previous design projects is a significant advantage in the design of new products.

- *Downstream costs*. When the design team modifies a product design, there is a good chance that it will cause modifications in other parts of the design, in a ripple effect. The only source of information for what these changes may be is the design team itself, which the accountant must regularly interview for clues about the cost effects of these changes.

- *Supplier performance data.* Suppliers are likely going to provide a significant proportion of the components of a new product, so the accountant needs access to the company's database of supplier performance to see if key suppliers are capable of supplying goods within the performance constraints required by the new design. This is less of a cost issue than a qualitative review of the ability of a supplier to perform within the company's specifications.

Clearly, the accountant must have access to a broad array of data sources in order to be a fully functioning member of a design team. These data sources frequently do not contain the high degree of data accuracy that the accountant needs, so the result is likely to be a significant degree of uncertainty in costing information, especially during the initial stages of product design.

## The Product Life Cycle and Target Costing

Target costing generates a significant and immediate cost reduction at the beginning of a product's life cycle. Kaizen costing then generates an ongoing series of smaller cost reductions that gradually decline as the number of cost reduction opportunities are eliminated. A company that wants to stay competitive with its product offerings should carefully track the gradual decline in product costs, and replace the original product with a new one when there are minimal cost reductions still to be garnered from the old product. The new product is subjected to the same target costing approach in order to create a new value proposition for the consumer, to be followed by another round of kaizen costing.

In order to remain competitive over the long term, it is clear that a company must be aware of where its products stand within their product cycles, and be willing to replace them when there are minimal costs to be eliminated from the old designs.

## Summary

Target costing is most applicable to companies that compete by continually issuing a stream of new or upgraded products into the marketplace (such as consumer goods). For them, target costing is a key survival tool. Conversely, target costing is less necessary for those companies that have a small number of legacy products that require minimal updates, and for which long-term profitability is more closely associated with market penetration and geographical coverage (such as soft drinks).

Target costing is an excellent tool for planning a suite of products that have high levels of profitability. This is opposed to the much more common approach of creating a product that is based on the engineering department's view of what the product should be like, and then struggling with costs that are too high in comparison to the market price. Given the extremely cooperative nature of target costing across multiple departments, it can be quite a difficult change for the engineering manager to accept.

*　　*　　*　　*　　*

In this book, we have continually focused on improving profits, not sales. In many cases, it makes sense to walk away from low-profit customers, so that you can focus on those customers who are most willing to pay your prices without complaint. The result should be a smaller, more focused organization that sells properly-configured products at the right prices to those customers who appreciate them the most.

# Glossary

**B**

*Bundling.* When several goods and services are clustered together and offered for a single package price.

**C**

*Committed buyer.* Someone willing to pay a premium over the market price for a good or service.

*Constraint.* A restriction on the output of a system.

**L**

*Loss leader.* A product that is sold at a deep discount from its list price.

**N**

*Net profit.* Throughput minus all operating expenses.

**O**

*Operating expenses.* All company expenses other than totally variable costs.

**P**

*Price point.* A suggested selling price for a product or service, as defined by a manufacturer or retailer.

**S**

*Sprint capacity.* The excess production capacity located upstream from a constrained resource.

**T**

*Target costing.* When an organization plans in advance for the product price points, product costs, and margins that it wants to achieve.

*Throughput.* The margin left after totally variable costs are subtracted from revenue.

**V**

*Value pricing.* A strategy of setting prices primarily based on a consumer's perceived value of a product or service.

# Index

Bundling ................................................. 16

Charge for free services ......................... 11
Committed buyers ................................... 5
Constraint analysis ............................... 27
    Financial terms ................................. 27
    Model ................................................ 28
Constraint-based pricing, objections to 36
Cost reduction programs ....................... 41
Cost-based pricing ................................ 25

Discount avoidance ............................... 19

Long-term contracts ............................... 32
Loss leader adjustments ......................... 20
Low price constraint analysis ............... 31
Low-price mindset ................................... 4

Market capacity, monitoring of ............ 21
Market segmentation .............................. 7

No market constraint, pricing impact ... 34

Offering options .................................... 18
Optimum price point ............................... 3

Price administration ............................... 22
Price increase
    Breakeven volume ............................. 2
    Experimentation ................................ 12

Impact of ............................................. 1
Price modeling ..................................... 32
Price reduction techniques .................... 23
Pricing discussions, frequency of ......... 23
Pricing strategies .................................. 25
Product line pricing .............................. 16
Profit per customer ............................... 12

Senior management support ................... 1
Setup-based pricing .............................. 32
Strategic pricing .................................. 26

Target costing
    Data sources ..................................... 45
    Milestone reviews .............................. 41
    Overview of ...................................... 38
    Problems with ................................... 42
    Process steps .................................... 38
    Role in ............................................. 44
    Team members ................................... 43
Teaser pricing ...................................... 26
Throughput per minute .......................... 28
Transactional pricing adjustments ......... 10

Unprofitable customers, elimination of. 12

Value dissipation ................................... 9
Value engineering ................................. 40
Value premium ....................................... 6
Value pricing ..................................... 8, 26
Value pricing sales techniques ............... 9